Sermons For Pentecost III Based On Gospel Texts For Cycle C

Good News Among The Rubble

J. Will Ormond

CSS Publishing Company, Inc., Lima, Ohio

SERMONS FOR PENTECOST III BASED ON GOSPEL TEXTS FOR CYCLE C:
GOOD NEWS AMONG THE RUBBLE

Copyright © 1997 by
CSS Publishing Company, Inc.
Lima, Ohio

Scripture quotations are from the *New Revised Standard Version of the Bible*, copyright 1989 by the Division of Christian Education of the National Council of the Churches of Christ in the USA. Used by permission.

Library of Congress Cataloging-in-Publication Data

Ormond, J. Will, 1919-
    Sermons for Pentecost III based on Gospel texts for cycle C : good news among the rubble / J. Will Ormond.
       p.   cm.
    Includes bibliographical references
    ISBN 0-7880-1038-7 (pbk.)
    1. Pentecost season—Sermons. 2. Bible. N.T. Gospels—Sermons. 3. Sermons, american. I. Title.
BV61.075   1997
252'.64—dc21

96-46498
CIP

This book is available in the following formats, listed by ISBN:
    0-7880-1038-7   Book
    0-7880-1098-0   Mac
    0-7880-1099-9   IBM 3 1/2
    0-7880-1100-6   Sermon Prep

PRINTED IN U.S.A.

Dedicated to
the memory of
two minister friends of mine,
both of whom died much too soon:

Michael Gibson Fitch

September 30, 1952 — September 24, 1994

Peter Cameron Carruthers

September 9, 1947 — August 28, 1996

Editor's Note Regarding The Lectionary

During the past two decades there has been an attempt to move in the direction of a uniform lectionary among various Protestant denominations.

Preaching on the same scripture lessons every Sunday is a step in the right direction of uniting Christians of many faiths. If we are reading the same scriptures together, we may also begin to accomplish other achievements. Our efforts will be strengthened through our unity.

Beginning with Advent 1995 The Evangelical Lutheran Church in America dropped its own lectionary schedule and adopted the Revised Common Lectionary.

Reflecting this change, resources published by CSS Publishing Company put their major emphasis on the Revised Common Lectionary texts for the church year.

Table Of Contents

Foreword

"Ordinary Time" sounds so — ordinary. And it seems to stretch over vast sweeps of the Christian calendar. The periods between Epiphany and Lent and between Pentecost and Advent are called Ordinary Time. Does it mean mediocre, a little below average, run-of-the-mill, commonplace, mundane, general, everyday? Is Ordinary Time a period the church plods through as we wait for the more exciting times of Advent, Christmas, and Easter?

In liturgical terms "ordinary" means that which is standard, normative, usual, or typical. It is "ordinary" to have worship every Sunday. There are elements of worship which are repeated each Sunday, things like the Creed, the Doxology, the Lord's Prayer. These are called "ordinaries."

It is typical that a sermon is preached every Sunday. Of course, it is to be fondly hoped that it is not the same sermon each time. But the act of preaching is an ordinary part of Worship.

To call the sermons in the volume "Ordinary Sermons" is not to make a judgment on their quality. They are ordinary in that there is no particular theme which runs through all of them, except that they attempt to preach the gospel.

The style of most of them is what I call "interpretive retelling of the story."

It is my hope that whoever reads these sermons will find some new insight into the Scripture passage upon which the sermon is based. My further hope is that anyone who uses them will not use them "as is," but will put the preacher's own individual stamp upon them. That should make them extra-ordinary sermons.

J. Will Ormond
Atlanta, Georgia

Then There
Was One

Proper 23   *Luke 17:11-19*
Pentecost 21
Ordinary Time 28

$\mathbf{Does}$ not Jesus say to the ten lepers, "Go and show yourselves to the priests"? He does not say anything about coming
back to tell him what the priests said or did; he does not mention
that he expects the lepers to return and thank him for their healing.

Yet when one does come back to thank him, he asks, "The
other nine, where are they?"

The one who returns gives no answer to that question. But he
could have said, "They are following your instructions. They are
on their way to show themselves to the priests."

Down through the ages the nine non-returning lepers have been
condemned, ridiculed, and held up as glaring examples of insensi-
tivity and lack of gratitude. How many sermons based on this story
have been used to berate congregations for not being thankful
enough, especially at the Thanksgiving season?

But can we not say a few words in defense of the nine? They
do seem to be law-abiding citizens of their time. They travel in
groups, as was the custom for lepers. They stay at a safe distance
from other people so as to avoid the risk of spreading the disease.

The story takes pains to point out that the one who returns is a
Samaritan. Therefore, the nine must be Jews. But here they are

accepting a Samaritan into their group. They travel with him. They share their meager fare with him. Remember that in that culture Jews and Samaritans had nothing to do with each other.

Of course, it is their common despair which helps break down the ancient barriers among them. They are all outcasts, Samaritan and Jew alike. But the Jewish lepers could well have driven the Samaritan from their midst with harsh words, such as, "Leprosy makes us unclean enough without adding the uncleanness of this cursed Samaritan."

Can we not credit the nine with a measure of confidence, even of faith, in Jesus? They evidently recognize him, for they call him by name. They address him as "Master," a title usually reserved by Luke for use by disciples. "Jesus, Master," they cry in a loud voice.

Their request, "Have mercy on us," can be interpreted at its lowest level as an urgent plea for alms. But Jesus does not so interpret it. He knows that the greatest expression of mercy for these tragic souls is to heal them.

I wonder if all ten are not somewhat puzzled when Jesus says simply, "Go and show yourselves to the priests." He does not touch them as he has done with other lepers. He does not pray over them. He does not declare them cleansed.

But the implication is clear. There were elaborate Old Testament rules for the cleansing of lepers. Going to the priest was the last step in the ritual. The priest did not heal the leper; rather the priest confirmed the cure. It was necessary for the priest to declare the leper healed so that the person could return to society and to a normal life.

It seems to me that it takes some measure of faith for the lepers to begin their journey to the priests while the marks of leprosy are still on their bodies.

We do not know how far they travel before someone begins to notice a dramatic change in their condition. Perhaps one feels a sensation like a cooling breeze on his parched skin. He looks at his hands. They are smooth and free of sores. He lifts his robe and examines his legs. No longer are they disfigured and discolored. They appear as sturdy as they were when he was a youth.

He gives a great shout. "My leprosy is gone! I am clean! I am clean!"

Then all the others with great excitement and anticipation examine themselves and find that all are cured. An almost overwhelming sense of wholeness sweeps over the group. They cry out in joy and wonder.

"The man said for us to go show ourselves to the priests. Hurry, let us run like the wind so we can be declared healed and return to our former lives. Come on. Let's get going!"

They take off down the road as fast as their legs will carry them. Their one thought is to reach the priests and be set free.

That is, all but one. One stands in the road transfixed. His mind goes back to the man to whom he pled for mercy. He is immersed in a tingling sea of gratitude. "The priests can wait. I must go back and thank the one who made me clean."

It may be that since this one is a Samaritan he is not as concerned about following the letter of the rituals as are his Jewish companions. Since he is considered a heretic would he go to the same priests as do the others? Perhaps he does not feel himself as bound by the law as do his friends. Perhaps he is of a freer spirit than are they.

In any case, his joy and gratitude overwhelm his strict obedience to Jesus' command. While the others are rushing to the priests, the Samaritan is eagerly retracing his steps to the place where he first met Jesus.

His is no silent, contemplative journey. We can imagine him running, leaping, perhaps singing as he praises God with a loud voice. Immediately he recognizes that the source of his healing is the mercy and power of God, and he gives joyful expression to that fact.

This time as he approaches Jesus he does not remain at a distance. He rushes to him and falls prostrate at Jesus' feet in humble gratitude. We are not told what words he uses as he thanks his benefactor, but surely he pours out a torrent of joyful wonder and praise.

Jesus responds to the healed leper's paean of praise with three questions. These questions seem addressed not so much to the Samaritan as to whomever has ears to hear. "Were not ten made clean?" "But the other nine, where are they?" "Was none of them found to return and give praise to God except this foreigner?"

Jesus expects no answer from the Samaritan himself. The questions are left hanging in the air for all to hear. Then Jesus adds a benediction and a blessing to the Samaritan's joy. "Get up and go on your way; your faith has made you well."

This is the second command the Samaritan has heard from Jesus this day. Both include the word "Go" — "Go and show yourself to the priest" and "Go on your way." The first restricts the man to a particular route and a specific goal. The second recognizes his new freedom.

Do you suppose the man ever goes and shows himself to the priest? The story does not tell us one way or the other. But we can be sure that the nine complete their ritual journey. Without a doubt, they appear before the priests and are declared clean. And then what?

They have obeyed Jesus' command. They are now well. Their story has a happy ending. But their story is incomplete. They have no idea what they have missed. If they ever again encounter their former companion, the Samaritan, he can tell them what is lacking in their story. He can tell them about a newfound freedom which lives not by the strict fulfilling of rules, but goes beyond obedience into joyful gratitude. He can tell them that while their bodies may be cured, their spirits can fully live only through praise, worship, and gratitude to God.

For us rule-keeping, upright, churchgoing Christians this story of the ten lepers is not a simple "sweet little story." The question which haunts us is: "The other nine, where are they?"

Perhaps some of us can say, "I attend church regularly. When I say the Apostles' Creed, I am sure I believe every word of it. I pay my pledge, usually on time. Occasionally I volunteer for the night shelter." But is that enough?

Where is the exuberant praise, the extravagant gratitude, the wild, joyful freedom in living, the willingness to go beyond what is required?

You know, I wonder what it would be like in my daily living to be motivated entirely by thanksgiving to God. My guess is that it is a great deal more freeing than always asking, "What is expected of me?"

The only way I am going to find out is to try it.

"Hey, Mr. Samaritan, wait for me."

An Extremely
Odd Couple

Proper 24   *Luke 18:1-8*
Pentecost 22
Ordinary Time 29

There are only two characters in this short parable which
Jesus told to his disciples. One is a man; the other, a woman. But
what an odd pair they are. It is difficult to imagine a more striking
contrast between two people than that between the judge and the
widow.

Neither is named, but their very titles suggest the contrast.

"Judge" calls to mind authority, power, representative of the
law, dispenser of justice.

"Widow" in the culture of Jesus' time suggests helplessness,
humility, poverty, vulnerability, loneliness, isolation.

One would expect, then, that in any conflict between the two
the widow would not stand a chance. We would expect her to make
her plea timidly in a trembling voice, and then at the first roar of
the judge's resounding "No" to slip unobtrusively away into the
shadows.

But not this widow!

She keeps coming back to the judge's court. It is not likely that
she brings with her an assortment of high-priced lawyers. It is
doubtful that she comes into court with an armful of law books or
stacks of briefs and precedents. I cannot imagine her raising her

15

voice or pounding the table. Nor can I see her with downcast eyes nor hear her whimpering her request through piteous tears.

The only line she is given in the story is a straightforward, legitimate request: "Grant me justice against my opponent."

We are not told who her opponent is nor what injustice she has suffered. But she seems to have no advocate, and her status as a widow makes her easy prey for a variety of unscrupulous characters. Her case is probably like many the judge hears every day. It may seem unimportant to the judge, but it is of crucial concern to her.

Between her and justice is the judge sitting on his high bench in his somber robes. From him she has a right to expect vindication for her situation.

But not from this judge!

He is characterized as one who "neither feared God nor had respect for people." He himself acknowledges this assessment of his character.

Since he does not fear God, the judge feels no compulsion to make proper moral judgments. He has no sense of accountability to an authority higher than his own. He is a law unto himself; therefore, he can make rulings which are arbitrary, judgments based on his own whims.

Since he has no respect for people, one can hardly expect compassion from him. When he sees the widow standing before him and listens to her request, he does not see a person in need of justice. He regards her only as an annoyance, only another petty nuisance, not worthy of his time. He can easily dismiss her with no pangs of conscience at all.

What weapons does she have against such an adversary? Surely her arsenal is empty and she stands helpless before the judge.

But not this widow!

Her weapons are those for which the judge has little respect or understanding because he does not possess them himself.

Among her weapons are patience, persistence, integrity, a strong sense of justice, and confidence in the rightness of her cause. She has the faith to believe that at the end of the day right will win out over wrong, justice will triumph over injustice, good will conquer evil.

Day after day she comes to the judge's court with her request: "Grant me justice."

Day after day he ignores her. Time and again he will not consider her case. The judge is sure that eventually she will give up.

But not this widow.

Did she become discouraged? I am sure she did. Did she ever wonder whether she had a ghost of a chance to break through this judge's hard and callous shell? Perhaps. Was she ever on the verge of becoming bitter because of the treatment she was receiving from this powerful man? If so, one could hardly blame her. Did she ever consider giving up?

Not this widow!

How long she keeps coming to the judge we are not told. But one day he looks up from his bench, and there standing before him once again is the widow.

Can't you see him putting his head down on his desk, and wailing in a plaintive voice, "Oh, no, not again, not again"?

The judge does not undergo a sudden change of character. He does not experience a dramatic conversion. He admits that still he does not fear God nor respect people. But at long last he grants the woman justice.

His motives have nothing to do with morality or compassion or concern for the oppressed. His motives are self-centered and cynical.

He has discovered that this widow, for all her seeming helplessness, is a formidable woman. Somehow he has to get rid of her. She is like a burr under his saddle, a pebble in his shoe. His reason for granting her justice is: "This widow keeps bothering me, so I will grant her justice, so that she may not wear me out by continually coming."

It is for his own protection, his own peace of mind, his own comfort that he finally makes the decision which he should have made when the widow first appeared before him.

Luke gives this parable an introduction which suggests why and to whom it was first addressed.

"Jesus told them a parable about their need to pray always and not to lose heart."

Jesus is speaking to people who have been taught to pray and who do pray. But these same people may well be in danger of "losing heart."

There must have been times when Jesus' contemporary followers were in danger of losing heart because of rejections, lack of understanding on their own part, and the sheer weary routineness of the road.

This story about a helpless widow who by patience and persistence prevails over a ruthless judge should give them courage for the long haul. It should bolster their resolve to continue in patient and persistent prayer. Surely it was a great source of hope for those first Christians.

Many of them held on to hope. Many of them never wavered in their faith. Many of them showed incredible patience and were persistent in prayer. Had they not done so, the Christian church would not have survived.

This parable not only encouraged them to be patient, but it gave them a basis for their hope.

Ironically, they could see in the character of the judge the basis for their hope. They grasped the truth that God is not like the judge. Jesus himself makes the point by posing a question which sets the character of God in stark contrast to that of the judge: "Will not God grant justice to his chosen ones who cry to him day and night? Will he delay long in helping them? I tell you, he will quickly grant justice to them."

God does not have to be cajoled, pestered, hounded or worn down before he will hear the cries of his people. If a ruthless judge will finally and grudgingly respond to patience and persistence, how much more will God?

Throughout the ages the people of God have had to wait with patient and persistent faith for God to act to give them justice.

Think of the children of Israel enduring slavery in Egypt for hundreds of years before God sends Moses to Pharaoh, an unjust tyrant, to demand, "Let my people go!"

Again and again Moses and Aaron go to Pharaoh to plead for the release of the slaves. Over and over the king of Egypt refuses. Then after a series of plagues Pharaoh relents. He lets the people go, not because he has finally developed a sense of justice and compassion, but because these people are about to wear him out. He wants to get rid of them.

Come to more modern times and think of the civil rights movement. Remember the African-American slaves of recent centuries singing spirituals in the cotton fields of the South. They took up the cry of the Hebrews in Egypt, "Go down, Moses. Tell old Pharaoh, 'Let my people go.' "

With persistence and patience they continued to pray and hope for freedom and justice. There were many times when they could cry to God, "How long, O Lord?"

But at last in the middle of this century things began to change. African-Americans finally won a measure of freedom and equality in this country. They were granted the right to vote in places where that right of citizenship had long been denied; they no longer had to sit at the back of the bus. They were no longer barred from certain restaurants and schools.

Of course, full and complete justice has not yet been attained by the descendants of former slaves. There will always be need for patient, persistent prayer and pressure in pursuit of justice. Faith in the faithfulness of God makes such patience possible.

Jesus knew that through the coming ages there would be times when his followers would be tempted to lose heart. At the climax of the age would they still be holding firm?

Therefore, at the conclusion of the parable he poses a question which gives promise of his final return and challenges his disciples of every age to pray always and not lose heart.

"When the Son of Man comes, will he find faith on earth?"

We cannot avoid this question for ourselves by projecting it far into some vague, remote future. It faces us here and now. Surely the unnamed widow of Jesus' gripping story can encourage us to continue to trust God to deal with us graciously in whatever circumstances come to us.

We need not fear to struggle with God in prayer. We need not be hesitant about bringing all our needs, doubts, and fears to God. For when God sees us coming God never wails, "Oh, no, not again, not again." God invites us to keep on coming.

The Beginning
And The Ending

St. Luke, Evangelist   *Luke 1:1-4; 24:44-53 (L)*

Some people, when they pick up a new book, look first at the beginning and read a few lines, then they turn to the end to see how it turns out. This gives them a preliminary feel for the book and helps them decide whether they want to read it or not.

We are faced with something of the same situation by the lectionary passages chosen for today. They are the first four verses from the Gospel of Luke and the last ten verses of the last chapter. We are asked to consider the beginning and the ending of Luke's gospel. The passages are the preface, Luke 1:1-4, and the summary at the end, Luke 24:44-53.

I am sorely tempted to ask the entire congregation to open your Bibles and read the whole Gospel of Luke at one sitting. I suspect this is something few of us have ever done before. But to do so would give us an overall impression of the entire Gospel. It would help us grasp something of the wholeness of the story and sense the beauty and power of Luke's themes and motifs. We could be impressed with the uniqueness of Luke's narrative, especially that which Luke records that we do not find anywhere else in the New Testament.

But we can learn a great deal about the Gospel of Luke and its author by considering the beginning and the ending of the book.

Luke begins his gospel in an entirely different manner than any other gospel writer. He begins with a well-crafted preface which establishes his qualifications as a reliable writer and gives something of the purpose of his book. Many writers in the first century A.D. began their works with a preface similar to Luke's.

Luke's preface is one long, elegant, well-balanced Greek sentence. Such a sentence would catch the eye of an educated reader and establish Luke as a person with literary skills who knows how to write history.

Luke acknowledges that he has used written sources which are based on eyewitness accounts. He has also done scholarly research by investigating "everything carefully from the very beginning."

The subject matter of his research is "the events which have been fulfilled among us." Luke writes as a member of a community which was brought into being by the events to which he is about to bear witness. These events are a fulfillment of long-awaited promises of God.

Luke states the purpose of his writing: "so that you may know the truth concerning the things about which you have been instructed."

As was often the custom in the ancient world, Luke addresses his book to a particular person, "most excellent Theophilus." Such respectful address may imply one of high rank, perhaps a Roman official of some kind. Theophilus already knows something about the Christian faith, for he has been "instructed in" or "informed of" the significant events. Luke wants to emphasize the truth of what Theophilus already knows, and he will add a great deal which Theophilus has not yet heard.

Theophilus may be Luke's patron who will see to it that Luke's work is published and distributed. "Theophilus" means "friend of God." Anyone who helps preserve Luke's great story is certainly God's friend and ours.

But of course Luke is not writing for the benefit of Theophilus alone. He has a much wider audience in mind. He echoes the message of the Christmas angel, "I am bringing you good news of great joy for all the people" (Luke 2:10). Luke is both historian and evangelist. He wishes to spread the good news of Jesus Christ far and wide.

Surely anyone who reads Luke's preface is eager to move on into the book to hear about the things that have been fulfilled and about which Luke has done such careful research.

Now let us look at the end of the book and see what it has to tell us about the story of Jesus and the motivation for spreading the good news.

The passage at the end of the Gospel is made up almost entirely of words of Jesus. But this is the risen Christ speaking. The crucifixion is past and the reality of the resurrection has just burst in upon the startled disciples. Amazement, joy, and wonder almost overwhelm them as they see their crucified Master standing among them risen and alive.

His voice reaches back over the whole sweep of the story Luke has been telling. "These are my words that I spoke to you while I was still with you." The risen Christ, although transformed, is the same person they followed from Galilee to Jerusalem.

Surely these words bring back memories of the early days in Galilee as Jesus went from place to place teaching, calling followers, doing mighty works, and ministering to the poor, the blind, the oppressed, and those on the margins of respectable society, such as prostitutes and lepers.

The disciples remember the day when Jesus decides to set his face to go to Jerusalem (9:51). He deliberately chooses the journey to the Holy City and nothing can deter him from his goal. Luke uses the motif of a travel narrative to emphasize that Jesus is moving ever nearer to where he will fulfill his destiny and complete his work.

The disciples surely recall the last days before the crucifixion when Jesus taught daily in the Temple and debated with the religious authorities. These same authorities continued to press him until at last they persuaded the Roman governor, Pilate, to have him crucified.

The principal thing Jesus now wants his disciples to understand is that his life and ministry is rooted in the Hebrew Scriptures. In his gospel Luke emphasizes from the beginning that the story of Jesus is a continuation, a fulfillment, of God's dealing with God's people in history. Jesus makes the claim that the whole of Scripture — the law, the prophets, and the Psalms — is fulfilled in him. In order for the disciples to grasp this significant truth, Jesus helps them read their Bible in a new way, "He opened their minds to understand the scriptures." He wants them to see that there is continuity between the mighty acts of God recorded in the Old Testament and the things they have seen in the life, death, and resurrection of Jesus Christ.

The days immediately before and including the crucifixion had been a difficult and puzzling period for the disciples. It must have seemed to them that God's plans had failed and that Jesus' ministry among them had gone for naught. But Jesus shows them that all that has happened is a fulfillment of scripture. "Thus it is written, that the Messiah is to suffer and to rise from the dead on the third day."

The entire story Luke has told has most significant consequences. Jesus tells the disciples "that repentance and forgiveness of sins is to be proclaimed in his name to all nations, beginning from Jerusalem." Here is the good news. People are offered the opportunity to repent and the gift of forgiveness is available to all peoples. The fact that the spread of the message begins from Jerusalem is further evidence that the Christian gospel is rooted in and grows out of God's saving acts on behalf of Israel. Jerusalem is the symbol of the foundation of the faith of Israel; from there the message will extend to the whole world. Luke, the evangelist, sets no limits on the boundaries for the gospel.

Now Jesus lays the responsibility for spreading the message on the disciples themselves. Since they are witnesses to the things which have been fulfilled among them it is up to them to tell the good news.

A formidable task indeed, but Jesus gives them a promise that they will receive a power far beyond their own strength. "I am sending upon you what my Father promised; so stay here in the city until you have been clothed with power from on high." They are to wait in faith and patience until it is time according to God's schedule.

Now we see that there are only a few more lines in Luke's gospel. There is no room to tell about the coming of this power from on high. Therefore, we want to know more.

Now the scene shifts its location. Jesus takes his disciples outside the city as far as Bethany and pronounces a benediction upon them. Then Luke recounts in one single brief sentence one of the most mysterious scenes in the story of Jesus. "He withdrew from them and was carried up into heaven."

This sentence, too, arouses our interest and makes us want to know more. But the symbolism is clear. Jesus is now exalted to the highest place of power and authority. He shares the glory of God. His work on earth is completely vindicated.

The disciples seem to have no sense of loss as Jesus leaves them. They worship him and return with joy to the Temple in Jerusalem where the first scene in Luke's gospel is laid. There the priest, Zechariah, had heard the joyful news that his aged wife, Elizabeth, would bear a son who would "make ready a people prepared for the Lord" (Luke 1:17). The story has come full circle.

Luke completes his story, but not his book. Luke cannot write "The End" on the last page. A much more appropriate phrase is "To be continued," for the conclusion is open-ended. We have already noticed how Luke's gospel cries out for a sequel. And Luke does not disappoint us. In the book of the Acts of the Apostles he continues the story. There we find a fuller account of Jesus' ascension into heaven. We see the promise of the coming power fulfilled when the Holy Spirit descends on the gathered company on the day of Pentecost. We find many stories of the disciples fulfilling their role as witnesses to all nations. They move from Jerusalem, the center of Judaism, to Rome, the center of the world of that day.

I dare to hope that this look at the beginning and the end of the Gospel of Luke has stirred your interest and aroused your curiosity to the point that you can hardly wait to get home and read the entire book from beginning to end. Can you think of a more profitable way to spend a Sunday afternoon?

When Self-esteem
Gets Out Of Hand

Proper 25   *Luke 18:9-14*
Pentecost 23
Ordinary Time 30

Once I had a friend who was offended whenever the phrase "we are miserable sinners" was used in the corporate prayer of confession. She did not feel that she was a *miserable* sinner. And indeed she wasn't in comparison to most of the other people in the church. She was compassionate, kind, thoughtful, and a great teacher of little children in Sunday School. Nor did she "regard others with contempt" — or at least, not many others.

I don't think she liked the phrase in an old hymn, "Would he devote that sacred head for *such a worm as I?*" She thought such phrases as "miserable sinner" and "such a worm as I" did nothing to enhance one's self-esteem.

I suppose she had a point. We are much concerned about having a healthy sense of self-esteem in regard to ourselves, and especially for our children if we are parents, or our students if we are teachers. This is as it should be.

There are people who have an extremely low sense of their self-worth. Often they try to compensate either by an obnoxious false bravado or an unctuous Uriah Heep groveling humility. Such people need help in raising their sense of self-worth. But this sermon is not addressed to this group, except, perhaps, in an oblique kind of way.

But can self-esteem get out of hand at times? The apostle Paul gave this warning to the Roman Christians and to us: "I say to everyone among you not to think of yourself more highly than you ought to think" (Romans 12:3).

Jesus must have known some people whose self-esteem had gotten out of hand and turned into self-righteous arrogance. He addressed this parable "to some who trusted in themselves that they were righteous and regarded others with contempt." Their sense of self-worth had taken the bit in its mouth and dashed down the road out of control.

Ironically, one such person revealed the extravagance of his self-esteem in the house of God and in an act of worship.

A Pharisee went up to the temple to pray, a commendable act indeed. It is well to go often to the house of worship. An indispensable part of worship is prayer. But the motive for worship and the manner of prayer are all important.

For this Pharisee both his posture and the tone of his prayer revealed his self-righteousness.

One translation (NRSV) says that he was "standing by himself." Another (RSV) has "he prayed thus within himself."

Both these phrases are highly revealing. If he was standing by himself it suggests an aloofness from other worshipers, especially any whom he considered unclean.

If he was praying "within himself," then he was carrying on a conversation with himself rather than communicating with God.

But he did want God to overhear what he was saying. He wanted God to know that he was thankful. "God, I thank you...." That seems to be a good start for a prayer. Don't we often begin a prayer with "O God, I thank you for all your many blessings" without being too specific about what those blessings are?

But this Pharisee was quite specific about the things for which he was grateful. He was grateful for those things which he thought set him apart from and above other people. "God, I thank you that I am not like other people."

Then he began to list the ways in which he was different. He evidently had a low estimate of his fellow human beings, for he lumped them under a list of disreputable characters: "thieves, rogues, adulterers." He singled out one of his temple companions as a special example of someone whom he was glad he was not like — "even this tax collector."

A tax collector in the minds of most law-abiding Pharisees was at the bottom of the moral, ethical, and religious totem pole. Such an assessment had good basis in fact. Tax collectors were often notoriously dishonest. They were looked upon as traitors to their own people because they worked for a foreign occupying power, the Roman Empire. They had a reputation for greed and for defrauding the poor. Therefore, the tax collector was an excellent foil for the paraded piety of the Pharisee.

Notice that the Pharisee spent the first part of his prayer telling God what the Pharisee was not. The whole list was negative. He did not thank God for any positive characteristic which he possessed. He wanted credit for himself for not being like other people, especially the tax collector.

But at the end of the prayer he put forth a list of two things he did regularly which he was sure God approved. Both were "religious" acts: fasting and tithing, both of which he performed beyond the minimum requirement. "Look, Lord, I am extra good."

Not once did the man mention compassion, or kindness, or service to others. He never said, "I helped a poor beggar who sat by the road," or "I gave some of my income to feed the poor," or "I volunteered at hospice to comfort the dying."

But if he had said any of these things, his self-esteem would still have been out of hand. Although his prayer was in the form of "thanksgiving," what he really wanted was God's confirmation that he was exceptionally righteous and therefore deserved God's acceptance. Surely, God was in his debt, not the other way around. There was no hint that he trusted in the mercy and grace of God; rather he "trusted in himself that he was righteous." His theology had no room for "salvation by faith alone." Perhaps he invented the old cliché, "It's not what you believe that counts; it's what you do." He could have added, "... and don't do."

Thus far we have almost overlooked the other character in this story except to say that he is in great contrast to the Pharisee.

He, too, went to the temple to pray. But his posture and actions showed no arrogance nor pride. Humbly he stood apart from those whom he knew were more righteous than he. He did not presume to look in the direction of God's dwelling place, but stood with downcast eyes. He beat upon his chest as a sign of remorse.

He was one of those people whose self-esteem was out of hand in a far different direction than that of the Pharisee. This man's sense of self-worth had hit rock bottom. He had good reason to feel miserable about himself, for he was a tax collector with all the disreputable baggage that weighed down the position. But he looked at himself honestly and made no excuses for his numerous misdeeds.

He prayed briefly, earnestly, sincerely. He made no pretense of giving thanks. He had no list of good deeds that might cause God to look favorably upon him. Nor did he recite a long litany of specific misdeeds which he had committed.

One sentence was his prayer, but that one sentence showed more faith and more understanding of the nature of God than the Pharisee's self-congratulatory recital of his piety.

"God, be merciful to me, a sinner."

That was all. But it was enough. Jesus' verdict: "this man went down to his home justified rather than the other."

"Justified" — that is, accepted by God, made right with God, put in a just relationship with God.

But why? Why was a confessed sinner more acceptable to God than a person who kept the rules and observed the correct rituals of the faith? Doubtless many who first heard this parable asked that question.

The tax collector simply threw himself on the mercy of God. He took his own sin seriously. He knew that God is righteous, hates sin, and will bring the sinner to judgment. He knew he could not hide himself from God, and he had no virtues with which to mask his unrighteousness. But he had enough faith in God to believe that God could be merciful, even to him. He had nothing to offer; he had no ground to stand on except the undeserved grace of

God. He knew that salvation is not his doing, but that it is a gift of God. He was bold enough to ask for that gift.

Jesus summed up the parable with a saying which must have been a favorite of his, for we find it at the end of another parable in Luke (14:11). "All who exalt themselves will be humbled, and all who humble themselves will be exalted."

Now, where do I find myself in this story?

I could pray, "God, I thank you that I am not like this Pharisee, arrogant and self-righteous."

But then would I be much different from the Pharisee? Is being proud of my humility more acceptable to God than letting my self-esteem get out of hand?

But can I identify myself with the tax collector? Surely I am not that bad. I do consider myself a person of integrity. I am honest, and I do have some measure of compassion for others.

But wait a minute. Now I am sounding dangerously like the Pharisee who paraded his virtues.

I think I will go stand with the tax collector and join him in his simple prayer. "God, be merciful to me, a sinner." For while I may not be exactly like him, I do know I am a sinner who has no ground to stand on except the mercy and grace of God.

Come, let us go up to the temple to pray.

Walking
On Our Hands

Reformation Sunday   *John 8:31-36*

$\mathbf{For}$ weeks now the Gospel lectionary readings have come from the Gospel of Luke. But today we encounter an intruder. Our journey through the last chapter of Luke's story is interrupted by another Gospel writer, John, who drops us into the middle of a debate between Jesus and "the Jews."

It is well known that the Gospel of John differs in many ways from the other three Gospels. Robert Kysar's book on the Gospel of John is called *John: the Maverick Gospel*. This is how his introduction begins:

> *There is a delightful little film about a small boy who learned to walk on his hands instead of on his feet. The story is done in animation and stresses the pressures toward conformity in our society. The little boy's strange behavior had the most pleasant results for him. Walking on his hands gave him a radically different perspective on the world. He could smell the fragrance of the flowers without bending down. He was close to the earth where he could see vividly the beauty of grass, and he met the butterfly eyeball to eyeball as it skimmed along the ground.*[1]

Kysar concludes that the Evangelist John walks on his hands because he has a different perspective on the story of Jesus than do the other Gospels. Matthew, Mark, and Luke are known as the "Synoptic Gospels" because they "see together." They follow the same general outline of Jesus' story, and share much of the material with each other.

John, on the other hand, rearranges the synoptic chronology. For example, he has the cleansing of the Temple early in Jesus' ministry (John 2:13-22). The Synoptics place the cleansing during the last week of Jesus' life. John has Jesus going to Jerusalem at least three times; the Synoptics record only one such journey. John has no parables, but he has Jesus give long discourses, many of them dealing with Jesus' own identity. "I am ... the good shepherd ... the door ... the bread of life," and the like.

This characteristic of being a maverick, of nonconformity, makes John an appropriate Gospel to provide a text for Reformation Sunday, for the early reformers were the mavericks of their day. Luther, Calvin, Knox, and others who struggled against the rigidity of the church walked on their hands.

Of course, they did not suddenly decide to begin walking on their hands and lay the foundations for a new Church. They were faithful Christians and desired above all else to reform the Church according to what they believed was the biblical order of the community of faith.

Nor were they the first to challenge the status quo of the Roman Church. Others had preceded them. Some, like Patrick Hamilton of St. Andrews, Scotland, had given their lives for the cause. Finally Luther, Calvin, and Knox came to the point where they felt that they were compelled to walk on their hands.

Martin Luther walked on his hands when he nailed his 95 theses to the church door in Wittenburg and railed against the sale of indulgences, which was like obtaining forgiveness for a price. John Calvin walked on his hands when he wrote his *Institutes of the Christian Religion* in which he set forth his interpretation of scriptures and the Christian faith and criticized doctrines put forth by the Roman Church. John Knox walked on his hands when he preached boldly in St. Giles Cathedral, Edinburgh, and chided Mary, Queen of Scots to her face.

But the all-time champion of walking on one's hands is Jesus Christ himself. He walked on his hands all the way to the cross. He challenged all the powers that be: religious authorities, political powers, and many of the cultural mores of his time.

He nearly drove the priests and scribes crazy by healing on the sabbath and violating in other ways their interpretation of the laws of Israel.

He went around talking about the kingdom of God and implying that he himself was a king. This did not sit too well with the Roman authorities. For them the Roman empire was the only legitimate kingdom, and Caesar the supreme lord and king.

Jesus knew what some people said of him: "Look, a glutton and a drunkard, a friend of tax collectors and sinners" (Luke 7:34). Pharisees and scribes said, "This fellow welcomes sinners and eats with them" (Luke 15:2). Jesus stated the purpose of his mission: "I have come to call not the righteous but sinners to repentance" (Luke 5:32).

In the matter of the people to whom he ministered and with whom he associated, he walked on his hands. By doing so, he offended the respectable members of society.

Our Gospel Lesson takes us into the middle of a debate between Jesus and the religious authorities whom John often refers to as "the Jews."

One obvious point of contention in the argument is whose testimony is true or valid and whose is not. At the beginning of the debate Jesus says of himself: "I am the light of the world." His hearers counter: "You are testifying on your own behalf; your testimony is not valid." Jesus comes back with, "My testimony is valid because I know where I have come from and where I am going" (John 8:12-14). He then cites the law: "In your law it is written that the testimony of two witnesses is valid" (John 8:17).

Jesus states that the two witnesses in his case are the Father and Jesus himself. "I testify on my own behalf, and the Father who sent me testifies on my behalf" (John 8:18).

The most familiar phrase in the lectionary passage is "you will know the truth, and the truth will make you free" (John 8:32).

Freedom is such a precious commodity that it comes as something of a surprise that Jesus' hearers take offense at his offer of freedom. They must think to themselves: "Who does he think we are, a bunch of slaves in Egypt? And who does he think he is, Moses?"

They depend on their ethnic and religious tradition for their status. As descendants of Abraham they think they are already free. "We have never been slaves to anyone."

The tradition of being descendants of Abraham is a proud and valuable tradition which should not be dismissed lightly. Jesus himself is a descendant of Abraham. The first book in the New Testament begins: "An account of the genealogy of Jesus the Messiah, the son of David, the son of Abraham" (Matthew 1:1).

Commenting on our passage, Fred B. Craddock writes:

> *Tradition gives security, direction and identity. Tradition provides the narrative into which one is enrolled. Whoever cannot remember any farther back than birth is an orphan, dislodged in the world. Tradition provides an agenda for a community's life. Tradition offers some criteria by which to evaluate the fads and claims of each generation. Tradition brings the past into the present, making the past alive and available and nourishing ... One does not relinquish tradition easily.*[2]

But Jesus' opponents had perverted their tradition. It had become hardened and impervious to change. It served the past rather than being open to the present and the future. They had become slaves to the very system they claimed as the source of their freedom.

Their fierce loyalty to their descent from Abraham had enslaved them. Since they believed that physical descent from Abraham was all that was needed to put one into right relationship with God, their ears were deaf to Jesus' call to discipleship. They did not recognize his word as coming from God the Father. "If you continue in my word, you are truly my disciples ... There is no place in you for my word. I declare what I have seen in the Father's presence" (John 8:31, 37-38).

In John's gospel the greatest sin is unbelief in Jesus as the Son of God. These arrogant descendants of Abraham were already slaves to that sin. They were plotting to kill Jesus. Later in the debate Jesus said to them: "Your ancestor Abraham rejoiced that he would see my day; he saw it and was glad ... Very truly, I tell you, before Abraham was, I am" (John 8:56, 58). Unlike his descendants who were enslaved by the past, Abraham was always moving toward the future. He was open to God's surprises like the birth of Isaac and the coming of One who was the fulfillment of all the promises God had made.

Reformation Sunday is not a time to pillory the Pope nor to bash the Catholics. It is not a time to proclaim "We are descendants of Luther, Calvin, and Knox, and have never been slaves to anyone."

Rather it is a time to recognize and celebrate our heritage and traditions as Protestants. A vital part of that recognition and celebration is to have the same openness to further reformation, growth, and change, as did our ancestors in the faith. Our foundation is still secure and solid, based unapologetically on the Word of God and the revelation in Jesus Christ.

As the writer to the Hebrews puts it: "Therefore, since we are surrounded by so great a cloud of witnesses, let us also lay aside every weight and the sin that clings so closely, and let us run with perseverance the race that is set before us, looking to Jesus the pioneer and perfecter of our faith, who for the sake of the joy that was set before him endured the cross, disregarding its shame, and has taken his seat at the right hand of the throne of God" (Hebrews 12:1-2).

Is that not an invitation to a wild and exhilarating freedom? "If the Son makes you free, you will be free indeed" (John 8:36).

1. Robert Kysar, *John: the Maverick Gospel* (Atlanta: John Knox Press, 1976), p. 1.

2. Fred B. Craddock, *John, Knox Preaching Guides* (Atlanta: John Knox Press, 1983), p. 67.

Topsy-turvy
Christianity

All Saints' Day   *Luke 6:20-31*

$\mathbf{Do}$ you know anyone who is financially well off and secure, who has an abundance of things and often dines in the best restaurants, who enjoys life and has a good time, and who is well thought of in the community? You may be such a person yourself, but if not, wouldn't you like to be? In such a situation we could declare that life is good, that we are content, and that the future looks bright.

Do you know anyone who is poor, hungry, grieving, hated, excluded, reviled, and defamed? I sincerely hope you are not such a person. We consider anyone who has all these woes as an extremely unfortunate individual indeed.

And yet, did you hear the words of Jesus as recorded in the passage we read from the Gospel of Luke? "Woe to you who are rich ... Woe to you who are full now ... Woe to you who are laughing now ... Woe to you when all speak well of you...."

"Blessed are you who are poor ... Blessed are you who are hungry now ... Blessed are you who weep now ... Blessed are you when people hate you, exclude you, revile you, and defame you...."

What is going on here? Doesn't Jesus have it all upside down? This sounds like topsy-turvy Christianity to me.

Suppose you had been among the crowd who first heard Jesus speak these words. What do you think your reaction would have been? That might depend on the part of the gathered company to which you belonged.

According to Luke's chronology Jesus, just before he began this Sermon on the Plain, chose from among his disciples twelve whom he called apostles (Luke 6:12-16). These words must have come as a shock to them. Did some of them wonder what they had gotten themselves into? Did they ask one another, "Does he mean if we are poor we are blessed, but if we are rich we have woe?"

Perhaps Peter, a poor fisherman, turned to Matthew, a wealthy tax collector, and said, "See, the Master says I am the blessed one, but you're the one who is in trouble. How do you figure that one out? Is being poor supposed to make me happy, and are you miserable because you are rich?"

In any large gathering of people there are bound to be those who are grieving for one reason or another. Were there those that day with tears running down their faces? Did they wonder, "When are we going to laugh? The hurt is too deep, the wound is too sore for me to think about being merry. Does this man mean that I am happy because I am weeping? These are not tears of joy. They are tears of grief."

Since Jesus appealed to the outsider and the oppressed, there were doubtless those in the crowd who were excluded from respectable society, who were hated by others, who were reviled. Did they ask themselves, "Is he saying that we are supposed to leap for joy because we are outcasts? What difference does it make if the prophets of old were treated in the same way as we are? Does that make us prophets?"

Do you suppose there were any rich people in the crowd that day? Perhaps not, but there might have been. People came from all over the country as far away as Jerusalem, Tyre and Sidon. Many people were drawn to Jesus because they had illnesses for which they sought healing. Rich people can get sick, too, you know. Others may have come not from a sense of need but out of curiosity.

What did the rich people think when they heard all those woes pronounced on them? To say the least, they must have felt uncomfortable. Some of them may have become angry and left the crowd in a huff, mumbling to themselves, "I'm not listening to any more of this stuff. The man is a revolutionary and heretic."

These words of Jesus may not arouse such reactions today. Their sharpness has been dulled by familiarity or by a kind of casual attitude toward scripture. "Oh, that's in the Bible, and was spoken a long time ago in a culture different from ours. It is far too impractical for our time."

The Lucan beatitudes and woes are certainly at variance with the accepted criteria of our time concerning what it takes to make one healthy, wealthy, and wise. They also do not fit a theology which presents the gospel as a sure road to success, peace of mind, and easy forgiveness. These sayings leave little room for "cheap grace" which emphasizes the grace and mercy of God, but gives little attention to the moral demands of the Word of God.

We need to remind ourselves that these beatitudes and woes were never meant to be rules for the ordering of political life. They have to do, rather, with the kingdom of God.

There is no glorification of poverty, hunger, grief, nor persecution in Luke's version of the beatitudes. One is not exhorted to seek these negative positions in order to obtain a blessing.

There is no glossing over the reality of present distress. There is no call for stoic endurance. But hope is held out that wrongs ultimately will be righted and that God has a particular concern for the poor, the hungry, the grieving, and the victimized. Such concern is an important characteristic of Jesus' mission and of the kingdom of God. According to Luke's chronology Jesus' inaugural sermon in the synagogue in Nazareth was based on a passage from Isaiah which begins: "The Spirit of the Lord is upon me, because he has anointed me to bring good news to the poor" (Luke 4:18).

The poor whom Jesus is addressing are lacking in material goods. Some of them have "left all and followed him." They are living under the reign of God. In spite of their outward circumstances, they have a security which no amount of riches can give them.

Jesus also reminds them that those who serve God are often misunderstood, abused, and reviled. Such was the treatment of many of the prophets of old; therefore, the poor among Jesus' disciples are following a noble heritage.

But what of the rich, the satisfied, the lighthearted, the well thought of? For what reasons are woes pronounced upon them? They can so easily become self-satisfied and feel that they are deserving of their good fortune. They can get caught up in things as they are and see no need for change or growth.

People who seem to have everything going for them can easily glide into a sense of false security, which leads them to give scant attention to the future. Luke records some sayings of Jesus and a parable which speak to this attitude.

"One's life does not consist in the abundance of possessions" introduces the parable of the rich fool whose land produces a bumper crop. He boasts that he has ample goods laid up for many years. Therefore he can "relax, eat, drink, be merry." But that very night he dies. "So it is with those who store up treasure for themselves but are not rich toward God" (Luke 12:15-19).[1]

The Lucan woes do not condemn the "good things of life," such as wealth, abundance of goods, joy, and a good reputation. But they do warn of the danger of trusting in these things as a source of security in life. They are all transitory. Riches cannot compare with "treasure in heaven." Abundance of food may be taken away by illness or famine. Sorrow is bound to come into any life no matter how well protected. People praise false prophets because they tell them what they want to hear and do not challenge their false securities.

If the Blessings and Woes of the Sermon on the Plain turn our priorities topsy-turvy, what follows continues the process. Jesus gives a list of ethical precepts which go against every common sense natural impulse about how to get along in this world.

Here comes Jesus talking about loving our enemies and doing good to those who hate us; about blessing those who curse us and praying for those who abuse us. What is this about turning the other cheek? When someone hits me, am I not expected to hit back? If I am robbed of my topcoat, am I supposed to chase the thief down the street shouting, "Wait a minute! Here is my shirt. Take that too?" Am I supposed to give something to every beggar who shakes a tin cup under my nose? When someone robs my house, am I not allowed to call the police to see if the burglar can be caught and my stuff recovered?

Retaliation, getting even, standing up for our "rights," protecting what is ours — these are the standards by which most of us live. Jesus' radical precepts make us extremely uncomfortable, but they set forth the principles by which life in the kingdom of God is ordered.

> *Followers of Jesus may be victims, but they are not to regard themselves as such, being shaped and determined by the hostilities and abuse unleashed on them. Rather, they are to take the initiative, not by responding in kind, or by playing dead, or by whining. They are not to react but to act according to the kingdom principles of love, forgiveness, and generosity. Such behavior ... is a pursuit of that life one learns from God who does not reciprocate but who is kind even to the ungrateful and the selfish (v. 35).*[2]

I can see why this passage is appropriate for All Saints' Day. Anyone who comes close to living up to the standards of life in the kingdom of God should surely be called a saint. But remember, we are all "called to be saints," a call issued by Paul to the church in Corinth (1 Corinthians 1:2). But that church had many people whose lives did not perfectly reflect the precepts of Jesus' Sermon on the Plain. Still Paul called them to be saints. If we listen closely, that call comes to us as well.

"It is a precarious, risk-filled existence, but one the text calls 'blessed.' "[3]

---

1. Fred B. Craddock, *Luke, A Bible Commentary for Teaching and Preaching,* Interpretation Series (Louisville: John Knox Press, 1990), p. 90.

2. Charles B. Cousar, *Texts for Preaching, A Lectionary Commentary Based on the NRSV* — Year C (Louisville: Westminster John Knox Press, 1994), p. 617.

3. *Ibid.*

One Bride
For Seven Brothers

Proper 27   *Luke 20:27-38*
Pentecost 25
Ordinary Time 32

You are middle-aged or older if you remember when the movie *Seven Brides for Seven Brothers* was first released. It was an exuberant, fast-paced musical about seven brothers on the frontier of the United States who were all looking for brides. Such "commodities" were rare in their part of the world. But, of course, in the end each brother got his bride.

The story in our lectionary passage for today is about one bride for seven brothers, but the end of the story is not as happy and upbeat as was the movie.

The story is part of a "knock-down, drag-out" debate or argument between Jesus and some of his most powerful opponents. It takes place in the temple court in Jerusalem during the last week of Jesus' earthly life.

Although Jesus is immensely popular with a great many people, opponents have dogged his steps almost from the beginning of his public ministry. The opposition comes to a head and moves toward a climax as Jesus approaches Jerusalem, boldly riding a donkey and being greeted with shouts of "Blessed be the king who comes in the name of the Lord!" (Luke 19:38).

45

He heads straight for the Temple and takes it over as the arena of his activity in Jerusalem. One can imagine that the religious authorities are not too pleased with this turn of events.

Jesus teaches every day in the Temple. The tension between him and the authorities continues to mount. This is how Luke describes the situation: "The chief priests, the scribes, and the leaders of the people kept looking for a way to kill him; but they did not find anything they could do, for all the people were spellbound by what they heard" (Luke 19:47-48).

In such an atmosphere, conflict is inevitable. There is attack and counterattack.

The representatives of the establishment question Jesus' authority to rearrange the furniture of the Temple or to teach in its confines.

He counters with a question they cannot answer and a story which makes them extremely uncomfortable.

The authorities call in reinforcements. They send spies to listen to Jesus' teaching in the hope that they will hear some heretical or treasonous word by which they can accuse him to the Roman governor. These spies seek to bait Jesus with fawning compliments. Then they ask him a trick question about whether it is lawful to pay taxes to the government.

Such a question can raise strong differences of opinion in almost any age or country. It is an especially sensitive issue in the time of Jesus. If he says an unadorned "Yes," many of the common people who are on his side will be offended. If he replies "No," the Roman IRS will go into action against him.

Jesus' clever counterattack involves a Roman coin and the admonition, "Give to the emperor the things that are the emperor's, and to God the things that are God's" (Luke 20:25).

"Well, let's bring in the heavy artillery. Let's trap this traveling teacher with a complicated theological question based on scripture. Let's watch him squirm as he tries to get out of this one."

The Sadducees enter the fray. Many of them are aristocratic, arrogant, and wealthy. They accept as scripture only the first five books of the Bible, which they attribute to Moses. In these books they find no evidence for life after death and certainly no basis for a belief in a resurrection.

We can almost see them snickering behind their hands as they pose their questions in the form of an absurd hypothetical story about one bride for seven brothers.

The Sadducees are using an old trick. Instead of putting forth strong evidence for their own position, they are seeking to make Jesus look ridiculous and his beliefs seem absurd.

They raise the question of resurrection from the dead. Their story is based on a law in Deuteronomy which says that if a man dies childless his brother is to marry the widow and raise up children in his brother's name.

In the Sadducees' story, there is a family of seven brothers. In succession each brother marries the same woman, but each brother dies without fathering a child. Finally the woman herself dies.

The Sadducees now ask the question which they are sure is the clincher: "Whose wife will the woman be in the resurrection?"

I suppose those who ask the question have in mind a ridiculous picture of a family feud in heaven in which seven brothers argue about whose wife this woman was.

"I saw her first. I was married to her before any of you gave her a second look. All of you married her only from a sense of duty, but I loved her. She is mine."

"But I was married to her longer than any of you. I admit I married her out of a sense of duty, but I came to love her dearly. We had a wonderful life together. I am sure she prefers me above all of you."

"As far as I'm concerned, any of you can have her. In my household she was a disruptive presence. I did not like her very much and we never got along. This will not be heaven to me if I have to live with her as a wife through all eternity."

With his answer Jesus wipes out this chaotic scene. The Sadducees have no idea what resurrection is all about. They are unable to look beyond this present world and time into the possibility of a new dynamic future. They think of the resurrection as a simple extension of how things are now and here.

Jesus assures them that the resurrection belongs to a new and radically different age. In this present time, marriage is necessary in order to preserve the human race. One generation passes away like the grass of the field. For another generation to arise, there must be families in which children are born.

But in the resurrection, marriage is not necessary. There is no death. Life is not interrupted by the passing of one generation to make room for the next.

Those who experience the resurrection are like angels. Jesus does not say they become angels. Like angels they do not die any more. They are in the presence of God forever. Jesus calls them "children of God" and "children of the resurrection." Rather than owing their lives to earthly parents they have been given new lives by God.

The Sadducees base their question on a passage from one of the books of Moses. Now Jesus uses the same tactic. He brings into the debate a passage from another book of Moses. His opponents accept these books as authoritative scripture. If they accept the part about a man marrying his brother's widow, then they must accept the story of Moses and the burning bush.

Moses is alone in the wilderness. He sees a bush that is burning but is not consumed. A voice comes out of the bush telling him to put his sandals off his feet for he is standing on holy ground. Then the voice says, "I am the God of your father, the God of Abraham, the God of Isaac, and the God of Jacob" (Exodus 3:6).

I am sure the Sadducees accept this story as literal truth. But do they think through the implications of God's words at the bush? Jesus gives those words an interpretation his adversaries never considered.

If God identifies himself as the God of patriarchs long since dead, what does that say about the relationship now between God and those heroes of the faith? Jesus declares that God is not the God of the dead. God is God of the living. Death does not separate God from God's people. Abraham, Isaac, and Jacob have not disappeared from God's care and presence. They are "children of the resurrection," "for to him all of them are alive."

Are the Sadducees convinced by Jesus' interpretation of scripture? Do they change their minds about the resurrection? The story does not tell us, but I doubt it. Their feet are set in the long-since hardened concrete of their system. They are trapped in a rigid and unbending stance from which they choose not to escape.

But the more pressing question is: Do some of us have concepts of the resurrection life which need clarifying by Jesus' interpretation of scripture?

I have a friend who says he hopes heaven has a large video room where he can see any place in history at the height of its glory. He is especially interested in seeing Corinth and Ephesus when Paul was in those cities.

Jesus' word that God is the God of the living does not satisfy our curiosity about such things as a video room in heaven, but it does give us strong assurance that God does not abandon us at death. It may not make entirely clear what our relationship will be to those whom we loved dearly on earth but who have gone before us into the new age. But it does confirm that our relationship with God is forever.

No matter what the Sadducees think about it, from Jesus' point of view the one bride and the seven brothers are all content in the presence of God for eternity, and the question of whose wife she is never comes up.

Good News
Among The Rubble

Proper 28   *Luke 21:5-19*
Pentecost 26
Ordinary Time 33

The family heard the tornado warning on the radio. They turned on the television; the radar map showed the storm was headed for their town. The wind picked up and rattled the windows. The sky became dark.

They went out on the front porch and looked at the sky. And then they saw it: a funnel cloud swaying along the ground like a hungry elephant's trunk sucking up everything in its path.

They made a run for it — the father, the mother and two small children. They lay flat in a nearby ditch. They heard the roar of a freight train, which is the characteristic sound of a tornado. The rain came down in torrents. Small tree limbs rained down upon them. Then they heard a loud crashing noise as if something big was being torn apart. The father dared to raise his head and look up. To his dismay, he saw the roof of their house fly over the ditch and plunge into a grove of trees nearby.

In what seemed like an eternity, but was only a few minutes, the storm passed, the wind died down, the rain stopped, the sky began to clear, and an eerie silence settled around the huddled family. Slowly they climbed out of the ditch. They were shaken and soaking wet but thankful none of them was hurt.

"Where is the house?" six-year-old Amy asked.

In place of the house there was a desolate empty space against the sky. All the family could see was a pile of bricks with not one brick left upon another. Wooden beams were piled helter-skelter like so many oversized matchsticks casually dropped by a giant. Pieces of clothing hung at half-mast from trees left standing but stripped bare of their smaller branches.

"It is nothing but a pile of rubble," mumbled the father.

The family huddled together, hugged each other and cried.

"Where are we going to live? Where is all our stuff? This makes no sense," shrieked ten-year-old Andy.

Nobody offered an answer.

Slowly they moved toward the wreckage of their home. Despair and disbelief crept across their faces. For a while they simply stood there. They had no words.

Then Amy cried out, "Where is Kitty Cat? I've got to find Kitty Cat!"

Amy began to pick up small pieces of debris. She turned over broken boards. All the while she called, "Kitty Cat! Kitty Cat! Come here, Kitty Cat."

Her mother watched sadly and thought to herself, "She will never find that cat. It is either crushed under all this rubble, or it has been blown away over the fields. Amy loved that cat. She will be devastated."

Just then Amy heard the faintest little mewing sound coming from among the rubble.

"Kitty Cat! Kitty Cat! Where are you? Where are you?"

Kitty Cat, wet and bedraggled, came struggling from under a broken board which was resting on some bricks. The board and the bricks had formed a little shelter which protected the kitten from being crushed or blown away.

Amy was ecstatic. She picked up the dripping kitten and cradled her in her arms. Amy's tears turned to joy. For her there was good news among the rubble. A living being which she prized had survived the destruction of a terrible disaster.

The entire family shared Amy's joy. In fact, the father suggested: "Why don't we give that cat a real name? Why don't we call her 'Hope'?"

Rubble in abundance comes to mind as we listen to the words of Jesus from Luke 21. Picture the magnificent Temple in Jerusalem lying in ruins, with not one stone left upon another.

There are predictions of wars and insurrections, of nations struggling against each other, of natural disasters such as earthquakes, famines, and plagues. Can you imagine the rubble scattered over the landscapes by these catastrophes?

There are predictions of emotional rubble produced by persecution from religious and political authorities, betrayal by family and friends, and an atmosphere of general hatred toward those loyal to Jesus Christ.

How do we react to these dire predictions of disaster? Do they frighten us and make us anxious? Do we echo the questions of the first hearers: "When? What are the signs?"

Or do we dismiss them as belonging to an ancient time? After all, the Temple was destroyed long ago. Wars, instability among nations, earthquakes, famines, and epidemics are characteristic of every age in history, including our own.

Persecutions because of one's religious faith stain the pages of the world's history through the ages. Although we in North America today do not face the severe persecution the early Church endured, anyone who exhibits a strong faith and seeks to live by the law of love may well face resistance, rejection, hostility, and ridicule from a complacent culture.

Whatever our personal reaction to these words of Jesus, we can be overwhelmed by the rubble and miss the good news. But if we look closely enough we can discover open places through which hope, like a surviving kitten, emerges into the sunshine.

In the face of all the disasters in our world, we ourselves may feel like frightened kittens. But the good news tells us of One who is like a lion, majestic and triumphant over the rubble.

When Jesus predicted the destruction of the Temple and his hearers anxiously asked when this would take place, he calmed their fears by telling them to beware of false Messiahs who would come and announce that the end was near. "Do not go after them," he warned. In the face of fanaticism he encouraged an attitude of calmness and trust in God.

Among the rubble of wars and natural disasters, Jesus speaks these encouraging words: "Do not be terrified; for these things must take place first, but the end will not follow immediately."

How often in Scripture does God proclaim to a fearful people: "Do not be afraid"? When Moses led the children of Israel out of bondage in Egypt, the first obstacle they faced was the Red Sea. As the Israelites camped by the sea they heard the roar of chariot wheels and the pounding of horses' hooves. They looked back and saw Pharaoh's vast army bearing down upon them. "In great fear the Israelites cried out to the Lord" (Exodus 14:10).

Moses reassured them: "Do not be afraid, stand firm and see the deliverance which the Lord will accomplish for you today ... The Lord will fight for you, and you have only to keep still" (Exodus 14:13, 14). The waters of the Red Sea parted at God's command and the people crossed over on dry land.

When the shepherds in the field near Bethlehem were confronted by an angel and the glory of the Lord shone around them, they were terrified. But the angel said to them, "Do not be afraid; for see — I am bringing you good news of great joy for all the people: to you is born this day in the city of David a Savior, who is the Messiah, the Lord" (Luke 2:10, 11).

Often the "Do not be afraid" comes when someone encounters the presence of God in an unusual way and when God is about to do some remarkable thing for the good of God's people.

"These things must take place first, but the end will not follow immediately." These words surely calmed the fears of the first hearers, and they can be good news for us.

They imply that there is an orderly progression in history, that contrary to all appearances things are not out of hand. God is in control. Trust God.

Sometimes when catastrophes occur in our world or in our personal lives, we feel there is no future for us. Have you ever heard someone after the death of a child or a spouse cry out in agony, "My life is over. I have nothing to live for now"? In the midst of the rubble of despair the message of the Lord is, "There is a future which is in God's hands; the end is not yet. You are deeply hurt, but stand firm and wait for God's deliverance."

The prediction about Jesus' disciples being arrested, persecuted, turned over to synagogues and prisons, and appearing before kings and governors was literally fulfilled as the book of Acts vividly records. Surely such a prospect was not something to which they looked forward with joyful anticipation.

But Jesus gave them some good news related to the difficult times ahead. Rather than facing such persecution with dread, they were to see their situation as an opportunity to proclaim the name of Jesus Christ to people whom they may never have met if they had not been arrested and put in prison. "This will give you an opportunity to testify ... I will give you a word and a wisdom that none of your opponents will be able to withstand or contradict."

What a challenge and what a promise! Look for opportunities to bear witness to the Christian faith in the worst of circumstances. Many of us find it difficult enough to speak a good word for Jesus Christ when we are in a sympathetic situation, much less when the atmosphere is hostile. We feel that we don't know what to say. We are uncomfortable and hesitant. We fear failure.

Can we lay hold of the promise Jesus gave his first disciples? He told them not to worry about what they would say. He would give them the words. He would speak through them with such power that their opponents would be silenced.

It takes a great leap of faith to step out on these glimmers of good news among the rubble. But they can be gathered up in the faith that God never forsakes us and that nothing can "separate us from the love of God in Christ Jesus our Lord" (Romans 8:39).

The tornado may destroy the house, but if a kitten survives and crawls alive from under the rubble, there is hope for the future.

Food For The Body
And Food For The Soul

Thanksgiving Day   *John 6:25-35*

A $good$ many years ago in a certain theological seminary in the South there was a professor of theology who was the master of the pithy, memorable saying. He used to give young seminarians about to graduate this advice: "Marry as soon as possible and as often as necessary."

He had a classic table blessing which he used frequently, especially at public functions: "Lord, we thank you for food: food for the body and food for the soul. May we never lack for either and give us an appetite for both."

This blessing, it seems to me, sums up a healthy attitude toward nourishment, both physical and spiritual. It is certainly appropriate for use as we gather around our Thanksgiving tables today.

Feasting has long been an important element of our Thanksgiving traditions in the United States. In fact, for many people the Thanksgiving dinner is the be-all and end-all of the celebration. How many of us stuff ourselves at the table, and then spend most of the afternoon in a surfeited stupor on the couch in front of the television set?

This emphasis on food for Thanksgiving can and often does get out on hand, but food is surely one of the blessings for which we need to express gratitude. It is one of the necessities of life and a gift from God.

The passage which we read from the Gospel of John is part of a long discourse about food — food for the body and food for the soul. One of the characteristics of John's gospel is that it is difficult to isolate a short passage from its larger context. John's narratives and extended speeches are so intricately and closely woven that when we tug at one thread, the whole fabric begins to unravel. Therefore, in order to better understand our text we need to see something of the complete design.

The controlling motif of this long discourse of Jesus is bread. The event which sets in motion the weaving of the design is John's account of Jesus feeding the 5,000 in the wilderness. Loaves of bread dominate the story. Jesus himself raises the question of how Jesus and his disciples can buy enough bread to feed the multitude. Philip observes that six months' wages is not sufficient to buy bread so that each of this horde can get a bite or two. Andrew reports that there is a boy in the crowd who has five barley loaves and two small fish. Jesus takes the boy's lunch, gives thanks and distributes bread and fish to the gathered throng. All eat their fill and the disciples gather up twelve baskets of leftover broken bread.

Needless to say, the people are filled, not only with food, but also with excitement by this seemingly easy way to satisfy their hunger.

Jesus and his disciples leave the crowd and go across the Sea of Galilee. But the people hunt Jesus down and find him at Capernaum. They are puzzled about how Jesus got there and question him about when he arrived. This brings us into the threshold of our text.

Jesus immediately sees beyond the shallow motive of why the people are seeking him out. He also quickly makes a distinction between bread for the body and bread for the soul. The people enthusiastically follow Jesus across the Sea of Galilee not because they are committed to him or recognize who he is but because "you ate your fill of the loaves." They are interested only in food for the body. They fail to recognize that the food they received from Jesus' hands the day before represents far more than satisfying their hunger for one day.

Jesus reminds them that earthly bread does not last. A loaf of bread soon molds and decays. Although it satisfies one's hunger for a matter of hours, hunger pangs soon return and one must eat bread again and again.

He tells them about food that endures for eternal life. This food he himself will give them. He is authorized to do so by God the Father.

The people ask Jesus for some sign which will validate his promise. "They saw the signs he was doing for the sick" is the motive which brings the crowd to the place where Jesus gives them bread in the wilderness (John 6:2). But they do not grasp the significance of the signs which Jesus has already showed them. He tells them, "You are looking for me not because you saw signs, but because you ate your fill of the loaves."

John's conclusion of his account of the feeding in the wilderness is: "When the people saw the sign that he had done, they began to say, 'This is indeed the prophet who is to come into the world' " (John 6:14). Therefore, the sign does make a favorable impression on them. They see Jesus as an extraordinary person who can do remarkable things. They see him as one who fits the mold of some of the most important characters in their tradition.

In fact, they see some parallel between what Jesus did with the five loaves and what Moses did when their ancestors became desperately hungry in the wilderness on their way to the promised land. "Our ancestors ate the manna in the wilderness: as it is written, 'He gave them bread from heaven to eat.' "

The people refer to manna as "bread from heaven" but they evidently credit Moses with giving such bread to their ancestors. Jesus picks up on this phrase and takes it beyond the giving of manna and beyond the satisfying of physical hunger. He reminds his hearers of something they should already know. It was not Moses who provided the manna in the wilderness. It was God.

Jesus declares to the crowd that God the Father still gives bread from heaven. "The bread of God is that which comes down from heaven and gives life to the world." This saying arouses the interest of the people to the extent that they ask Jesus to give them this bread always.

59

What do they mean by "this bread"? How do they interpret "the bread from heaven"? Are they thinking only of an abundant supply of food which will never fail? Do they have visions of no more going to the market to buy bread; no more standing over a hot stove; no more anxiety about what they will eat or what they will drink?

Whatever they mean by "give us this bread always," their request opens the way for Jesus to tell them plainly what the bread of God which comes down from heaven is. His answer is a surprise to some and an offense to others. The remainder of his discourse on bread grows out of his answer.

What a bold claim Jesus makes: "I am the bread of life. Whoever comes to me will never be hungry, and whoever believes in me will never be thirsty."

The people had seen Jesus as a prophet like Moses who could supply them with food for the body. Now he is challenging them to see him as more than the supplier of bread but as the bread of God itself.

This claim of Jesus is not easy for many of the hearers to accept. Some say, "Is this not Joseph's son, whose father and mother we know? How can he now say, 'I have come down from heaven'?" (John 6:42).

Jesus takes the analogy of his being the bread of life even farther. He speaks of the necessity of eating his flesh and drinking his blood: "Those who eat my flesh and drink my blood abide in me, and I in them. Just as the living Father sent me, and I live because of the Father, so whoever eats me will live because of me" (John 6:56-57).

Such a strong and graphic figure of speech makes us uncomfortable. It was especially offensive to Jesus' Jewish hearers. We can sympathize with many of his disciples who said: "This teaching is difficult; who can accept it?" (John 6:60). Because of this difficult teaching "many of his disciples turned back and no longer went about with him" (John 6:66).

What can we make of this bold language Jesus uses to talk about bread for the soul? Is it a way of shocking us into taking our relationship to Jesus Christ extremely seriously? How close are

60

we to him? Do we relate to him as eagerly and intimately as we do to the abundance of food on the Thanksgiving table?

The human spirit has deep hungers which we often cannot identify. We try many ways to satisfy those hungers. We become workaholics and amass a fortune only to find that something still is missing. Perhaps we make a name for ourselves by great achievements only to come to the place where the praise of others sounds hollow. We travel the world to discover new wonders but finally lose our sense of wonder and one place begins to look as drab as another. In the last analysis, whether we recognize it or not, our ultimate hunger is for acceptance by and fellowship with God.

Jesus Christ offers us this acceptance and fellowship in himself. He invites us to believe in him whom God has sent. "This is indeed the will of my Father, that all who see the Son and believe in him may have eternal life; and I will raise him up on the last day" (John 6:40).

Just as the human body needs food to sustain life, so the soul, the essence of our being, requires food to promote life that has eternal quality. Such food must be everlasting and beyond the reach of decay and death.

Where can such food be found except in the life, death, and resurrection of Jesus Christ? When by faith we receive his life into our very being his life begins to nourish us and he abides in us and we in him.

There is one table at which the concept of partaking of his body and blood is not offensive to his disciples. It is when we gather at the Lord's Table and hear the words, "This is my body broken for you. This is my blood shed for you." Without hesitation but with joy and gratitude we eat the bread and drink the wine. Our souls are strengthened and our lives refreshed.

It is fitting and right that on this day we gather to give thanks to God for the abundance of material blessings which are gifts from heaven. It is appropriate that we enjoy food for the body and recognize it as one of God's most necessary gifts.

But our deepest and most heartfelt thanksgiving is reserved for the greatest gift of all, the bread of God which comes down from heaven and gives life to the world, the gift of Jesus Christ himself.

"Lord, we thank you for food: food for the body and food for the soul. May we never lack for either and give us an appetite for both."

The King
On A Cross

Christ The King   *Luke 23:33-43*

Have you ever looked into the face of a real king? You may have seen phony kings, such as the king of the homecoming parade or the king of the Mardi Gras. Doubtless these make-believe kings were dressed in elaborate, elegant robes and wore gilded crowns on their heads. If we ever think of kings we picture them sitting on golden thrones, dressed in ermine and velvet and jewel-encrusted crowns. They are surrounded by high-ranking courtiers and cheered by an adoring people.

Therefore, it can come as something of a shock to look into the face of a king on a cross. But that is exactly what the Gospel of Luke invites us to do.

This king has no gorgeous robes. He has been stripped of his meager clothes, and soldiers gamble for them at the foot of the cross. He is not surrounded by subservient courtiers nor adoring people but by a jeering mob and mocking soldiers. On his right and on his left there are no high-ranking functionaries but two criminals, each hanging on a cross.

But there it is for all to see, the inscription nailed securely to the top of the upright beam: "This is the King of the Jews." Here is an official government proclamation and indictment.

Is this some kind of cruel joke? Is this the governor's way of humiliating the Jews? How can such a powerless, pitiful figure be a king?

What brings this man to the cross is the recurring suspicion that he is a king. His enemies bring him before the governor and one of their accusations is that he has been "saying that he himself is the Messiah, a king" (Luke 23:2).

The governor asks him, "Are you the king of the Jews?" (Luke 23:3). The man does not deny the title. Since the governor can find no legitimate charge against the prisoner, he takes the phrase "King of the Jews" and makes that into the indictment.

The soldiers who are carrying out the crucifixion taunt the man with demands that he prove he is a king. "If you are the King of the Jews, save yourself."

Therefore, the inscription on the cross should come as no great surprise. Much preparation has been made for it.

Those who watch and those who take part in this execution think they are crucifying a person to whom the title "king" can be applied only in derision and jest.

But there is one character in the drama who has insight beyond the others. He is a most unlikely prophet. He too hangs on a cross. He is facing death because of serious crimes he has committed. He admits he is a sinner. He does not protest that he is being treated unfairly. But he sees in the man who is dying beside him one who is indeed a king.

This condemned man who recognizes the accused as the one who reigns over a kingdom is the lone voice raised in his defense. "This man has done nothing wrong." Then he makes an amazing request and a remarkable statement of faith. "Jesus, remember me when you come into your kingdom."

Somehow this man looks beyond all the evidences of defeat and powerlessness in which Jesus' adversaries revel. Where they see a vanquished enemy trembling on the edge of the abyss, he sees a royal figure exercising authority in most unexpected and radical ways.

What does he see, what does he hear that others are too blind and deaf to comprehend?

The three condemned men are lifted up on their crosses. Pain beyond expression surges through their bodies. Yet the man on the central cross prays, "Father, forgive them; for they do not know what they are doing."

What sort of person makes a prayer like this when he is dying in pain viciously inflicted by others? Should not such a one cry for help, plead for rescue, or even ask for a swift death? Is it not more appropriate for him to call down judgment and retribution upon those who take part in his execution than to pray for their forgiveness?

Perhaps the second criminal ponders questions such as these. Forgiveness is something for which he longs but does not expect to receive. But here is a man hanging beside him on another cross praying for forgiveness for those who execute him. What a strange strength is this! What a radical sense of mercy and justice! If he can ask forgiveness for those who kill him, perhaps he can ask forgiveness for me. Perhaps he can even grant it himself.

Now the compassionate criminal witnesses another development in the compelling drama. The powerful leaders of the people taunt Jesus and call on him to prove who he is. "He saved others; let him save himself if he is the Messiah of God, his chosen one!"

So the leaders admit that Jesus saved others. Therefore they grant him some measure of power. But in their minds if he can save others, surely he can save himself. How can the Messiah, the chosen of God, allow himself to stay on a cross?

The soldiers too join in the chorus of mockery. "If you are the King of the Jews, save yourself!"

It is the accepted wisdom of priests and soldiers alike that one who possesses power always uses it for his own advantage. Why be a king if you cannot prove it by spectacular demonstrations of force and might?

For Jesus these mocking words must bring back the echo of an earlier time when he is standing on the pinnacle of the Temple in Jerusalem and hears the voice of the Tempter: "If you are the Son of God, throw yourself down from here" (Luke 4:9). He resists such a temptation then, and resists it yet again.

But the criminal evidently sees in Jesus' refusal to bend to the demands of his powerful tormentors an authority which is not compelled to prove itself. Is there a greater act of authority, courage, and dignity than to refuse to save oneself in order to save others?

The criminal, with great effort, turns his head and looks again at the inscription on the central cross. "This is the King of the Jews." Perhaps he thinks, "They write better than they know."

His companion in crime hangs on a cross on the other side of the cross of the king. He is not impressed by Jesus' prayer for forgiveness for his executioners. He bristles when Jesus does not use his authority as Messiah to save all three of those who are condemned. If he has saved others then here is a chance to do it again. "Are you not the Messiah? Save yourself and us."

But the second criminal strongly rebukes his companion and reminds him: "We indeed have been condemned justly, for we are getting what we deserve for our crimes, but this man has done nothing wrong."

This man is given the insight to see the moral reality of the situation. He and his partner in crime are guilty sinners. They are bearing the consequences of their evil deeds. But Jesus is innocent. That very innocence enhances the regal authority of Jesus as he prays for his enemies and refuses to prove his power. Here is innocence suffering on behalf of guilt. Such understanding gives the confessing sinner boldness to make his confident request and to state his certain faith. "Jesus, remember me when you come into your kingdom."

This man believes that Jesus is not defeated but that he will be vindicated by God and ushered into his proper place in the divine scheme of things. He believes that Jesus reigns over a kingdom where forgiveness and pardon can be found and where condemned criminals like himself can find restoration rather than recompense. He greatly desires to enter into such a kingdom and be ruled by such a king.

Now hear the regal proclamation in response to the sinner's prayer and confession. "Truly I tell you, today you will be with me in Paradise."

Paradise is a symbol of a royal garden with cooling streams and lush trees bearing delightful fruit. Whatever its literal reality, it is in radical contrast to the present scene where three crosses stand beneath a merciless sun, where a milling, hostile mob watches without sympathy and soldiers laugh and gamble for discarded clothes.

Jesus promises the repentant criminal that he will be removed from such a scene and join Jesus himself in Paradise. Nor is this something that will come in the far distant future. "Today you will be with me in Paradise."

What a leap of faith it takes to believe such a promise, but the pardoned criminal has already confirmed his faith by recognizing a king on a cross. Therefore, he can trust the king to fulfill his promise.

On this day when the Christian calendar invites us to worship Christ the King, our attention turns to the cross as Jesus' throne and the crucifixion as the means of his exaltation.

Through his ministry Jesus proclaimed the Kingdom of God and declared that it was near. He told parables to set forth some of its characteristics. He invited those of humble, childlike faith to enter it. He warned the self-righteous that they were far from the kingdom. He acknowledged that his kingdom was immensely different from the kingdoms of the world.

Early in Luke's account of Jesus' ministry, Jesus in a sermon in his hometown of Nazareth sets forth some of the characteristics of his reign. He bases these on words from the prophet Isaiah. He declares that the Spirit of the Lord has anointed him "to bring good news to the poor ... to proclaim release to the captives and recovery of sight to the blind, to let the oppressed go free, to proclaim the year of the Lord's favor" (Luke 4:18-19).

Perhaps our most appropriate response to the vision of the King on a Cross is to hear the trumpet sound and listen to the loud voices in heaven which are saying, "The kingdom of this world has become the kingdom of our Lord and of his Christ, and he shall reign forever and ever," and to join the 24 elders in singing, "We give you thanks, Lord God Almighty, who are and who were, for you have taken your great power and begun to reign" (Revelation 11:15-17).

Alleluia! Long live the King!

Lectionary Preaching
After Pentecost

Virtually all pastors who make use of the sermons in this book will find their worship life and planning shaped by one of two lectionary series. Most mainline Protestant denominations, along with clergy of the Roman Catholic Church, have now approved — either for provisional or official use — the three-year Revised Common (Consensus) Lectionary. This family of denominations includes United Methodist, Presbyterian, United Church of Christ and Disciples of Christ. Recently the ELCA division of Lutheranism also began following the Revised Common Lectionary. This change has been reflected in the headings and scripture listings with each sermon in this book.

Roman Catholics and Lutheran divisions other than ELCA follow their own three-year cycle of texts. While there are divergences between the Revised Common and Roman Catholic/Lutheran systems, the gospel texts show striking parallels, with few text selections evidencing significant differences. Nearly all the gospel texts included in this book will, therefore, be applicable to worship and preaching planning for clergy following either lectionary.

A significant divergence does occur, however, in the method by which specific gospel texts are assigned to specific calendar days. The Revised Common and Roman Catholic Lectionaries accomplish this by counting backwards from Christ the King (Last Sunday after Pentecost), discarding "extra" texts from the front of the list: Lutherans (not using the Revised Common Lectionary) follow the opposite pattern, counting forward from The Holy Trinity, discarding "extra" texts at the end of the list.

The following index will aid the user of this book in matching the correct text to the correct Sunday during the Pentecost portion of the church year.

(Fixed dates do not pertain to Lutheran Lectionary)

Fixed Date Lectionaries *Revised Common (including ELCA)* *and Roman Catholic*	**Lutheran Lectionary** *Lutheran*
The Day of Pentecost	The Day of Pentecost
The Holy Trinity	The Holy Trinity
May 29-June 4 — Proper 4, Ordinary Time 9	Pentecost 2
June 5-11 — Proper 5, Ordinary Time 10	Pentecost 3
June 12-18 — Proper 6, Ordinary Time 11	Pentecost 4

69

June 19-25 — Proper 7, Ordinary Time 12	Pentecost 5
June 26-July 2 — Proper 8, Ordinary Time 13	Pentecost 6
July 3-9 — Proper 9, Ordinary Time 14	Pentecost 7
July 10-16 — Proper 10, Ordinary Time 15	Pentecost 8
July 17-23 — Proper 11, Ordinary Time 16	Pentecost 9
July 24-30 — Proper 12, Ordinary Time 17	Pentecost 10
July 31-Aug. 6 — Proper 13, Ordinary Time 18	Pentecost 11
Aug. 7-13 — Proper 14, Ordinary Time 19	Pentecost 12
Aug. 14-20 — Proper 15, Ordinary Time 20	Pentecost 13
Aug. 21-27 — Proper 16, Ordinary Time 21	Pentecost 14
Aug. 28-Sept. 3 — Proper 17, Ordinary Time 22	Pentecost 15
Sept. 4-10 — Proper 18, Ordinary Time 23	Pentecost 16
Sept. 11-17 — Proper 19, Ordinary Time 24	Pentecost 17
Sept. 18-24 — Proper 20, Ordinary Time 25	Pentecost 18
Sept. 25-Oct. 1 — Proper 21, Ordinary Time 26	Pentecost 19
Oct. 2-8 — Proper 22, Ordinary Time 27	Pentecost 20
Oct. 9-15 — Proper 23, Ordinary Time 28	Pentecost 21
Oct. 16-22 — Proper 24, Ordinary Time 29	Pentecost 22
Oct. 23-29 — Proper 25, Ordinary Time 30	Pentecost 23
Oct. 30-Nov. 5 — Proper 26, Ordinary Time 31	Pentecost 24
Nov. 6-12 — Proper 27, Ordinary Time 32	Pentecost 25
Nov. 13-19 — Proper 28, Ordinary Time 33	Pentecost 26
	Pentecost 27
Nov. 20-26 — Christ the King	Christ the King

Reformation Day (or last Sunday in October) is October 31 (Revised Common, Lutheran)

All Saints' Day (or first Sunday in November) is November 1 (Revised Common, Lutheran, Roman Catholic)

Books In This Cycle C Series

Gospel Set
Sermons For Advent/Christmas/Epiphany
Deep Joy For A Shallow World
Richard A. Wing

Sermons For Lent/Easter
Taking The Risk Out Of Dying
Lee Griess

Sermons For Pentecost I
The Chain of Command
Alexander H. Wales

Sermons For Pentecost II
All Stirred Up
Richard W. Patt

Sermons For Pentecost III
Good News Among The Rubble
J. Will Ormond

First Lesson Set
Sermons For Advent/Christmas/Epiphany
Where Is God In All This?
Tony Everett

Sermons For Lent/Easter
Returning To God
Douglas J. Deuel

Sermons For Pentecost I
How Long Will You Limp?
Carlyle Fielding Stewart, III

Sermons For Pentecost II
Lord, Send The Wind
James McLemore

Sermons For Pentecost III
Buying Swamp Land For God
Robert P. Hines, Jr.